# PISCES

# HOROSCOPE

## 2020

# *Pisces Horoscope*

# *2020*

Copyright © 2019 by Mystic Cat Press

## Pisces

**Pisces Dates:** February 19 to March 20
**Symbol:** Pair of Fish
**Element:** Water
**Planets:** Jupiter, Neptune
**House:** Twelfth
**Colors:** Purple, white

# JANUARY HOROSCOPE

## ASTROLOGICAL & ZODIAC ENERGY

INNOVATIVE ~ DECISIVE ~ PURPOSEFUL

## WORK & CAREER

You are entering a highly productive chapter, this may see you traveling or taking a course. You have a tricky goal to complete. It may be arduous getting this venture off the ground. You will have help from others to help provide you with a lucky break when you need it. Overall, the future is looking successful, you are being tested on several levels, but you have what it takes to overcome and shine. You have what it takes to accomplish your goals this year, though you will need to plan carefully. Your determination is on the rise, this enables a breakthrough and obstacles can be dealt with. You are deftly able to change gears and forge ahead towards prestigious opportunities. A new area is on the horizon, and this will draw happiness into your world. Talking with a friend helps you gain clarity and provides you with further information. You can expect a new rhythm which gives you productivity-boosting energy to go along with it. You settle into a comfortable and steady pace, which enables you to create security and stability. This is a great time to simplify and establish a path towards your goals. An endeavor you work towards begins to take concrete form, the improvement in your circumstances is headed toward long-term well-being. You are now ready to start creating a foundation which brings you serious results. You enter a vibrant time of developing your potential and are no longer resistant to change. A slow and steady pace creates a robust movement forward. This encourages you to reach for your goals as your dedication provides you with the motivation to achieve a perfect result. The ideas you envision dance in your mind to tempt you towards success.

## LOVE & ROMANCE

You can embrace the fond memories of the past. It has given you the courage to overcome hurdles and achieve your highest outcome. You see a path towards greater security, and you are taking steps to manifest abundance in your life. Adding in goals does allow you to see tangible results which reflect the changes you are making in your life. You are fully

4

supported in your efforts and will be allowed to grow towards a significant chapter which brings you joy. Heeding the call of your most cherished dreams does will enable you to hone in on achieving this goal. You are likely to be captivated by one who makes your heart sing. The seeds you plant towards developing your dreams blossom in the fullness of time. Taking affirmative action toward achieving your new life is highly favored and does provide you with a powerful proactive approach. This builds on your goals and gets you ready to embrace a fresh chapter. A friend from the past also may reach out this month, this one has hopes to team up with you once more. They seek in-depth conversations and a closer bond with someone who holds meaning to them. They are doing some research first to see if you may be open to a re-connection with them. They see it as tricky as it could lead to a delicate emotional situation. They have been going through a transition and are now focused on drawing abundance into their world. Someone is seeking to reveal their feelings to you. They hope to re-enter your life dramatically and expressively. They have much to say to you but hold back due to fear that their presence would be disruptive. There is a sense of secrecy, intimacy, and sharing of history together. They don't want to catch you off guard and hope to ease into this situation carefully. They feel deepening emotions could ensue after the right re-connection.


## IDEAS & CREATIVITY

There is an area which has been testing your patience, and it will resolve soon. This sees you being busy, as it is an excellent time to put things in motion. You have a solidly reliable chapter ahead, and this does allow you to achieve substantial goals. Your spirit is renewed and ready to face that which comes your way. With delays behind you, planning ambitiously for future growth is possible. News arrives, which is a welcome change of pace. An exciting opportunity is set to unfold. This is good news and takes you to a decision which is in alignment with your goals. You benefit from strategic planning, as this does bring valuable insight into your world. Your creativity is high, and carving out time to spend on passion projects is likely to result in a new enterprise. This is a path worth following upon. You can revisit a long-forgotten dream. This is something which creatively inspires, and you shall have luck on your side this time around. Your artistic side seeks expression. A hectic environment has led to excess activity, it is an excellent time to begin a slower pace and take it easy. An opportunity emerges soon to let your creative talents shine, you are set to achieve a great deal of success.

## ISSUES & HURDLES

Someone near and dear to you may prove to be a bit problematic, you find you have had enough of erratic behavior. You can release yourself from guilt if you do decide to pull back from this person for a bit. You're also likely to feel extravagant soon and splurge on an in-demand item. Experimenting with an activity you've always been curious about takes you on an investigation which tempts you on a new and diverse path. This is a great time to expand your horizons and seek new inspiration, you get a taste for what the future holds. Information is in hot demand, there is something coming which provides you with a cornucopia of choices. As you examine these options, you are presented with a symbol which speaks to your intuition. This connects you with the correct project to sink your teeth into.

There are more serendipitous and inspirational moments ahead, and this shines a light on the area of healing and rejuvenation. You do deserve a break, give yourself space to just merely focus on nurturing your inner child. Clearing your emotions will bring sustenance to your soul. There may be some baggage that needs to be released. As you head towards a productive chapter, your tenacity, resilience, and fortitude hold you in good stead. Sure, there are hurdles, life can be difficult, but improvement is at the crux of the energy which is flowing towards you. You enter a solid phase which allows transformation to occur, staying true to yourself, sees the situation around you changing and evolving. This sees you find a key which offers growth. This has been a chapter which provides pearls of wisdom. It does lead to personal growth, while you didn't ask to be put in this situation, you can create a shift which takes you to a happier chapter. Wrapping up the energy which limits progress does kick off a new cycle of potential. First, clear the decks and make space for a new power to arrive. Be honest about your situation, you know in your heart, the best is yet to come.

# FEBRUARY HOROSCOPE

## ASTROLOGICAL THEME & ZODIAC ENERGY

IDEALISTIC ~ VISIONARY ~ TENACIOUS

## WORK & CAREER

You enter a month for robust growth, which helps you get closer to a goal. You are productive and aiming towards bettering your circumstances. Epic messages arrive at inspiring you to keep moving towards your dreams. You get on a vital track which has terrific potential for future growth. An invitation out feels abundant and gratifying. This is music to your soul and provides you with unexpected downtime after a hectic month. You star burns brightly as you shimmer with potential. This month you achieve the culmination of a project you have been working towards, and this signifies that the changes you have put in place reach a turning point. This could deliver excellent recognition to you. Your skills and talents are noticed, bringing strong potential into your world. You also illuminate an area of growth and learning which holds potential for future progress. You have a strong will to accomplish your goals. This is taking you to a highly productive phase, and your efforts are seen by those who can assist you. It's going to take the initiative, but you had never been one to avoid hard work. A successful outcome is likely, and you find you are capable of turning the tables in your favor. Keeping this goal on your mind does bring up the chance for progression soon. A shift occurs which invites you to expand your horizons. You spend quality time with your closest family ties, and this connects you with a sense of grounded energy, which is essential in this beginning this new area. Spending time with your tribe does look inviting. It's a time of bringing the sun into your world and getting in touch with your emotions as you indulge in building stable foundations.

## LOVE & ROMANCE

Welcome news arrives, which gives you valuable insight into a situation which helps you reform your personal life and provides you with a surprising soulmate. Developing this situation does take you to profound change. Reviewing progress helps guide this path forward. Maintaining a sense of balance and flexibility is vital to obtaining natural growth. You are

7

blessed with a deep understanding of how to nurture fulfillment throughout this journey. You take an essential step towards developing a closer bond. This person provides you with emotional support and lets you see an optimistic side of life. Building strong foundations create sparks which hold helpful ideas for future growth. You enter a chapter which is emotional and focuses on deepening intimacy and joint ventures. This brings you to a turning point and pushes a personal relationship forward. You are set to launch into a new phase of potential. Anything started during this time is highly motivating. A fresh burst of wind propels the fire of inspiration within you. You may find yourself craving connections which hold a more profound element to them. Striving to communicate openly helps bring an intense bond center stage. This someone has traits which complement yours and together you can make things happen. The exciting potential is brewing in the background of your personal life. Expanding your horizons takes you to a chapter of personal growth. You enter a time which is ruled by social gatherings and lively discussions. Spending time with people you share common interests with as you craft a new endeavor. Support is available, this arrives and leaves you feeling optimistic. Seeing benefits in your life enables you to gain perspective and release stress.

## IDEAS & CREATIVITY

This is a month which highlights the expanded opportunity. You draw luck into your world, this allows you to benefit from improving social relations. There is an event which enables you to let loose and relaxes with kindred folk. Additionally, you have a busy month install, your talents going to be called upon, which provides you with a productive environment. It's a great time to generate new leads and focus on obtaining your best result. This is going to be the right path for you, it is a superb time to go into more delicate details. As you consider the options before you, you get a clear idea of how you want to give birth to this endeavor. All aspects that play into your higher vision should be considered. This provides you with a much more stable platform to build upon, it is a collaborative enterprise which relies on teamwork and frank discussions.

During the February 9 Supermoon in Leo, you follow a path of divinity and a higher calling. You have gifts which are currently untapped and should be developed as they can be a powerful ally towards bringing love and light into the world. This supermoon holds the key to compassion, it brings you in touch with your emotions and will play an unusually active role in your life over the coming months as there is an impressive total of 4 supermoons in 2020. The more you tune into it, the more you are aware that you are going in the right direction. This is a brilliant indication that ideas will arrive to help support growth. You can achieve a high result, which helps your situation. Radiating dynamically, you make headway on your goals. Working as a team brings you to sharing exciting plans with another. This highlights your ability to function under pressure and maintain a flexible outlook. Your epiphanies are set to blossom under a promising sky.

## ISSUES & HURDLES

The past has a strong influence over you, and rightly so. It is part of more substantial wisdom which surrounds your life. These are clues which guide you towards healing, and this is instrumental in allowing you to gain traction towards a future vision. The world of myth and symbolism also brews signs which hold meaning to you on a personal level. Gaining insight into your more profound wisdom provides you with impressive results. You are creative, you pull life-affirming potential into your world. Harnessing your talents correctly will enable you to create a path towards a higher level of achievement. Trust in your abilities, you have an area coming which will allow you to shine brightly. This sees you get accolades and recognition from others. As you make space to reflect on the changes which have arrived in your life, you can process some of the heavy emotions and deal with releasing outworn energy. You may take advantage of an opportunity which comes to tempt you out in the community. Making a leap of faith rewards you with new contacts who become valued friends, you meet someone who tempts you further. This enables you to transform your situation towards a vision which offers you grace and blessings. You make good progress on your goals, and this heralds you moving towards a happy a chapter. While development may feel slow at times, remembering you have support around, you will enable you to focus on achieving essential tasks which demand your attention. The little things add up for you this month.

# MARCH HOROSCOPE

## ASTROLOGICAL THEME & ZODIAC ENERGY

PROFICIENT ~ PRAGMATIC ~ CONSTRUCTIVE

## WORK & CAREER

It suggests significant change is afoot. Be discerning as you will be given several options to explore. This could be your key to emotional freedom as you release blocked energy, paving the way for a refreshing chapter of potential. A synergistic collaboration is likely and leads to developing a project which feels enticing. You immerse yourself in an inspiring area, it heightens your creativity and stokes the fires of your imagination. Increased stability is possible. This relates to systems of organization and a good solid plan which has practical results. Your visionary ideas will have a better shot of success if you plan and prepare to develop them methodically. As you expand towards achieving meaningful goals, you are provided with tangible progress. Fresh prospects arrive to guide your awareness and inspire you to keep forging ahead. An opportunity comes, which offers long-lasting security and recognition for the effort you put forth. It requires new levels of integrity, accountability, and personal responsibility. You lay the foundations for future progress, it does take the initiative to create a stable base which presents you with real opportunities for growth. Be patient with the process, you are being guided to achieve a successful outcome. An offer sweeps in with the potential to create a radical change, your work-life balance significantly evolves, this establishes a hot-spot of personal growth. A prominent role emerges which seems perfect for you. As you plant the seeds of potential, your life blossoms. Change is in the air, this is achieved through researching and strengthening your options. There are also opportunities for group activities which provide you with a welcome change of pace.

## LOVE & ROMANCE

You seek mutual bonds of balance and companionship. Exploring synergistic collaborations allows you to pay attention to the potential which seeks to emerge in your world. Singles can obtain a meaningful connection through expanding your horizons and drawing in new areas of growth and learning. Opportunity comes knocking later this year to tempt you out on your comfort zone. An enticing character stands out from the crowd at an event. You are a tender person, and that is what is so lovable about you. Your emotional intelligence is extraordinary as you can feel people's energy more than most. Intuitive and empathetic, you are always there for others. You will get a boost soon in the form of an opportunity which inspires you to enter a chapter of learning. You can expect to see progress in your life soon. An area which you have been working hard on is highlighted as suddenly moving forward. This good fortune can inspire you to keep striving to achieve goals. You are resilient, tenacious, and ambitious. The qualities of your spirit give you the strength to attain excellent outcomes in your world.

Couples find that compromising and making an extra effort to listen helps improve the most essential union. Someone significant surprises you with a thoughtful and romantic gesture. This puts the potential toward a long-term union. As your drive for poetic kinship intensifies, you become focused on nurturing a robust interpersonal bond with someone who captivates your attention and mesmerizes your imagination.

## IDEAS & CREATIVITY

You may feel a sense of restriction in your life's journey at present, this is guiding you to obtain enlightenment, getting to the bottom of what your soul desires will see you focusing your energy on an area which holds promise. Striving to deepen your understanding of your dreams puts you on the path to fulfillment. This is the perfect time to forge a new alliance. Your communication skills are on the rise, and this enables you to break through limitations and develop an essential bond with another. This aligns you towards having a meaningful conversation, speaking openly and from the heart does bring the potential to the forefront. The past has taught you many valuable lessons. It shapes the person you are today. The future offers you a myriad of possibilities, and this does reflect an overall path of self-development. You make decisive strides towards achieving an important goal. This relates to improving security, and it does provide you with a stable foundation from which to engage in speculative activities. Growth and learning are highlighted for you. Your past perseverance and dedication have provided you with a beautiful phase of growth. You are someone who sets a high standard and continually raise the bar of where you hope to be. You are likely to adopt a gentle approach in regards to nurturing yourself more and moving towards an area which suits your emotional needs. This could be getting more downtime and allowing your spirit to be rejuvenated. As you reboot, you find your goals shift.

## ISSUES & HURDLES

You are someone who can overcome hurdles and deal with life's problems succinctly. Page-turning new energy is coming, which will help facilitate a fresh start in your world. This brings you to an emotional time of improved well-being and highlights a growth-orientated chapter for you. After some reasonably hard times, you are ready for a change. A difficult decision has been made, you are doing what is best. You are thinking of all elements and factoring in what needs to be done to bring about the best outcome under these circumstances. This has resulted in more security and stability, which draws harmony in the environment. It creates the right conditions to thrive. The March 9 Supermoon in Virgo has the power to heal, it is likely to be a sensitive and emotionally aware event. This full moon in Virgo signifies letting go and moving on to a new area which is in alignment with your core values. A descent into your inner being, reflects insight and wisdom being bestowed upon your spirit to assist you on this journey. You may need time to process feelings and heal the past. Trusting in your inner voice sees you move in a new direction. You can move forward and achieve your dreams. Opening your heart to abundance sees beneficial energy flow into your life. Take time to pause, reflect, and make sure you are on your correct life path. You may find your priorities have shifted recently, focus on your foundations first.

# APRIL HOROSCOPE

## ASTROLOGICAL THEME & ZODIAC ENERGY

OPTIMISTIC ~ EXPANSIVE ~ IMAGINATIVE

## WORK & CAREER

You enter a productive time, which enables you to make robust progress. As you launch towards the achievement of goals, you influence another who provides you with valuable feedback. Information arrives to give you an idea of what is possible should you continue to work on developing a venture dear to you. It is an excellent time to connect with others, a beautiful moment makes an appearance which holds meaning to you. An opportunity arrives to provide you with additional work, this position rewards you with the potential for stability and growth. It is a hectic time, so remember to take a break, so you can recharge. There are lovely changes ahead that will work well for you, a new learning opportunity or course will be delightful for you. Your creative talents will shine, allowing you to get the recognition you deserve. Changes are coming, which will help to simplify your life, it will be grounding, allowing goals to take concrete form. Focusing on developing your potential sees improvement in productivity, this suggests security is likely to become the main focus, re-evaluating the plan leads to a stellar result. A significant turning point is shining a light on a substantial area to develop. A welcome surprise makes itself known to you soon. Once you overcome an excess workload, you find the path ahead is paved with golden opportunities. An area sparks your interest which holds plenty of potentials, you embark on developing this to its fullest outcome. You feel capable of making substantial changes which improve your circumstances. Hard work, dedication, and motivated heart are all that is required to achieve real success. News arrives, which provides you with valuable information.

## LOVE & ROMANCE

There is an emphasis on sharing ideas and thoughts coming into your world. You develop a closer bond with a kindred spirit you share communication with. It is the first phase of sharing and expanding your social activities. Setting your intentions enable you to use positive, progressive goals, this launches a precious period of increased harmony and abundance. You spend time with one who is thoughtful and philosophical, visionary, and idealistic. You're going to have plenty of newfound energy coming into your life soon enough, and this is going to have to do with love. You are getting ready to move ahead with what you feel to be best for your future; you're going to have a lot that you could investigate in the time ahead, as there's someone who's preparing to speak to you about their most profound feelings. You are ready to reveal you're real potential. The seeds you plant over the coming months have the chance to reap a magnificent bounty. This also corresponds with a new alliance heading into your life. The news of this partnership will begin to make itself known to you in ways which inspire and delight your awareness. It has the potential to become a critical element which brings you a great deal of happiness and harmony. You are a fantastic communicator. You soon are likely to reach a turning point with someone important to you, this creates a fabulous sense of connection. There is also a chance to reap the bounty of a new area which beckons your inspiration. This corresponds with a sense of adventure as it heralds the beginning of a new pursuit. Life takes on a grand vista of potential outcomes, significant change is now possible.

## IDEAS & CREATIVITY

The April 8 Supermoon in Libra takes you to a transformation which is profound and healing, this highlights a radical change which guides you towards becoming your highest potential. You may feel more aware of the connection between your thoughts and well-being as it can bring up the sensitivity, this allows you to utilize your intuition and gain a knowledge which is profound and mystical. Trusting in yourself takes you towards a heartfelt chapter of potential. Pay attention to signs as they are likely to arrive in your world during this lunar phase. This provides you with valuable information and enables you to spot an opportunity which becomes a turning point in your life. As you develop your world, you open fresh possibilities which are precisely in alignment with the correct direction for you. Slow-burning alchemy is simmering beneath the surface, providing you with sparks of inspiration. You enter an exciting chapter which highlights creativity and self-expression. As you make progress towards a future goal, you are aware that your efforts are providing you with tangible rewards. Original ideas are moving forward, this clears the deck for the new potential to arrive. Your dreams could be especially vivid during this time as your intuition is guiding substantial progress. A brilliant idea makes itself known to heighten potential. Your life undergoes a series of changes which revolutionizes your inner circle, this holds plenty of potential for your personal life. You have learned valuable lessons about obtaining balance and prioritizing your needs within a situation. Your next chapter sees passion and self-expression take a decisive stand. There are some beautiful opportunities around love and romance coming into your world. Clearing out old emotions and energy sweeps in this potential.

## ISSUES & HURDLES

You have been through a chapter of healing, closure, and release. This will allow you to traverse towards a better phase, less complicated one-on-one relationships are indicated, opening your heart to the potential possible reveals sweeter prospects. This type of personal expansion is perfect for you though it does come with some intensity, you can overcome nerves and release doubt. Thrilling encounters are indicated, more thrills in love are on the way. There is an opportunity ahead for you to connect in a deep and meaningful way with a person who holds your interest. Singles set aside solo tendencies and tune in to developing a closer bond with someone who sparks curiosity. This leads to an expansion in your inner circle and advances personal friendships, lifting some of the stress and heaviness, which may have been on your shoulders recently. Engaging in positive endeavors is a boost to your morale.

Additionally, you outgrow some people and move in a direction which feels more in alignment with your calling. There are so many ways to expand your horizons, reflecting on your life now will reconnect you with a path you may have put aside in the past, but now it feels the perfect direction to head towards. This boosts your desire for adventure, you can expand your current boundaries. You can be more open about your goals in life, especially in the matters of security and stability. You have tangible ways to reach a settled destination which grounds you in abundance. An event soon gives you a heartening glimpse of the potential possible, there are benefits of going deep and immersing yourself in a new area. You are set to benefit from an opportunity which will kick-start a new chapter for you.

# MAY HOROSCOPE

## ASTROLOGICAL THEME & ZODIAC ENERGY

GROUNDED ~ DEDICATED ~ EXPANSIVE

## WORK & CAREER

A significant epiphany could arrive soon, leading to opportunities to change your environment. Deep soul-searching creates an incredible atmosphere which rules closure, release, and healing. Ultimately, it leads to an expansive journey, which is positive and helpful. As you align your energy towards self-improvement, you obtain new heights of potential.

You shift towards developing your life to a higher level of achievement. Positive changes are arriving soon. You can bank on the fact that this potential is meant for you. Therefore it is essential to be aware a signpost is likely to emphasize which direction to explore. After all, your intuition does play a fundamental role in this process. With this in mind, spend time contemplating options, and you are likely to feel drawn to exploring a lesser-known path. It is time to consider planning for future goals. You find choices which lead to further improvements. There will be definite signs arriving later this year to continue to motivate you to keep on the path of abundance. There is also the potential for learning a new area which holds promise. This journey has elements for side progress, so it's not necessarily linear. Being proactive and taking the steps necessary is essential, you are drawing the right ingredients into your life. You are set to benefit from an improvement which inspires you to keep going. Change occurs over time. There is an opportunity coming which could yield significant results down the line. This heralds a fresh start, which gives you the chance to begin a chapter on a clean page. Turning over a new leaf as you adopt a lifestyle which lights the way towards improvement in your circumstances. As you rebuild and rejuvenate, you draw inspiration into your world. You move into a chapter which holds the promise of substantial growth.

## LOVE & ROMANCE

You are capable of enchanting a lover this month, this is a situation this person is drawn to developing. Only fear holds progress back. You are likely to deepen the bond with another, understanding the issues of your resistance to connection helps to refine the potential. Tinkering with your personal emotional outlook enables a more in-depth understanding to emerge. As you draw romantic abundance into your life, it is highly gratifying, and you can feel proud of yourself for the work you have done to reach this point. Overcoming stumbling blocks lead to a winning combination in love. Listening to your intuition sees you connect with a grander, more inspired vision. You see the big picture possible with another, and this leads to expansive potential. There is something special happening in your future. Adventure awaits you. Being open to new avenues and opportunities bring substantial potential into your surroundings. This kick-starts a glorious chapter with someone who has your heart. This is a time which places a focus on supportive and encouraging energy. It does set the stage to allow you to launch towards new heights of connection and passion with another. There may have been surprising plot twists and sparks with this person. Developing the relationship potential opens your heart to transform your world. Your focus is primarily guided by your intuition as you are highly sensitive and perceptive to this situation.

## IDEAS & CREATIVITY

This month calls for you to develop a delicate balance between your emotions and intuitive abilities. It indicates you improve the ability to balance creativity and artistic expression with knowledge and wisdom. This speaks of the connection between your inner voice and higher Self. You are a natural leader and can exude a sense of diplomacy and awareness to illustrate your emotions. A more full world calls your name, this is a prime time to connect with others in a social setting. Surrounding yourself with kindred spirits helps you embrace new innovative ideas and releases stress, drawing abundance into your world. You're likely going to find inspiration with others, this will add fire to your motivation, and see you expanding your horizons. Information arrives as you journey forward, which provides you with the motivation to keep developing your creative talents. You reach for your dreams. You enter a time of healing, endings, and release. This is leading you to a new phase of potential. Your creativity is highly activated, and you could receive important information as insights and bright moments of clarity. Pay attention to your intuitive side, as you are likely to feel a strong pull to a significant direction which is close to your heart. There may be a situation that you are uncertain about, clarity is achieved through spending time in quiet reflection. You will be assisted with

17

powerful ideas and insights. This enables you to realign your energy towards a direction which opens new potential and innovative solutions. By consciously focusing on refining your goals, dreams, and desires, you allow the most significant reward to enter your life while releasing that which has held you back.

## ISSUES & HURDLES

Understanding that phantoms of the mind do disturb your peace is part of the puzzle to solving this issue. Once you shine a spotlight on these restless vibrations you help release them to the universe, focusing on developing a strong core foundation enables you to have faith in the future, you can move forward knowing you are on the right path to support your vision. Releasing anxiety and doubt have always been part of a process of higher evolution. You may have been feeling frustrated recently by barriers in your life. This is a message from the universe to slow down and slow the pace, things likely to improve as a specific situation, most likely a romantic one is now beginning to move forward. The arrival of positive news provides improvement and opportunities to communicate on a deeper level. This gives you a sign that you can reflect upon. You are someone who embraces increasing the stability in your life, and this takes you towards achieving goals which are sumptuous and focused on your immediate environment. You are being guided to focus on the bottom line and see what changes can be instigated to make those improvements happen that you have been putting off. This could lead to a new creative path for you. You soon draw fresh inspiration which enables you to create a new way. Adopting a broader perspective does help tune your higher energies into an outlet, which will be the solution you have been looking for. It takes you to a phase of forgiveness, closure, and endings. You create space to heal unresolved pain through a process of grace which supports you at this sensitive crossroads. Moving forward draws you to a happier chapter.

# JUNE HOROSCOPE

## ASTROLOGICAL THEME & ZODIAC ENERGY

IMPULSIVE ~ PRODUCTIVE ~ ACTIVE

## WORK & CAREER

Stability is likely to be the outcome of your patience and flexibility. As you draw abundance into your surroundings, you can appreciate how far you have come on this journey. You are someone who has remarkable insights which allow you to be extremely sensitive to achieving your goals. This is a path which is built over time through developing experiences, as you fortify your foundations, this month does open the way forward. You are set to benefit from a new chapter. It shows that time of patience is required first, as you gather the right environment to create your next harvest. You are set to benefit from brushing up on skills, a new opportunity is likely to provide you with a breakthrough soon. Planning ahead puts you in the right arena to achieve success. Set your sights on long-term goals and work steadily towards obtaining your vision. You get the opportunity to see all the work you've been doing come together with a flourish. A change is indicated in which you step into a new role. This does spotlight heightened potential and gives you the motivation to ride a wave of success towards a busy time. It becomes a more productive time for you. You are reaching a time where there is a better match of characters entering your life. This sees you go through some changes. Heightened social opportunities arrive to encourage you to unwind with kindred spirits.

## LOVE & ROMANCE

This is likely to be a focused, intense chapter, it highlights an increasing sense of intimacy and emotional awareness. There is someone you explore deeper feelings with. You move out of your cocoon and let things flow forward as you travel through a time of heightened romantic potential. Pouring your attention into this connection creates security and stability. It becomes a significant confidence booster and allows you to shift towards happiness. You enter an extended time with this individual. This removes restrictions, and you begin to learn from each other's strengths. The combined energy which you create together is capable of developing

19

aesthetic goals. It is a bond which benefits from long-term planning and visionary ideas. This person sweeps in to create change in your world and can balance your emotions with their loving personality. Opportunities are ripe and full of possibility, this is a phase which is especially imbued with good fortune. You are industrious and productive, able to achieve substantial growth over the coming months. You are likely to be drawn to a romantic adventure, this leads to extended time, and you are rewarded for being proactive and bold. Chemistry is expected to guide your personal life, plan a moment which sizzles with potential soon. You enter a time of exceptional clarity, which provides you with a solution you can bank on. It is an especially potent time for developing personal bonds. You are likely to find adventure which sees you spread your wings and ride the crest of heightened inspiration. You are eager to seek out new horizons beyond your familiar zone, this leads to an expanse of opportunity. An in-depth conversation with another, taps into a desire for emotional harmony.

## IDEAS & CREATIVITY

There are definite indications are that you are drawing an exact romantic situation in your life. This provides a compelling opportunity for you to release the past and go after your dreams. As you gain a sense of self-mastery over your life, you embrace a character who makes you feel ready to take on the world. There is profound happiness suggested in the next chapter which unfolds in your life. Your life is set to reveal in meaningful ways. You capture the awareness of another who entices you out of your comfort zone. This person seeks to develop an emotional closeness with you but beware you may enter into the possessive territory. Allowing it to unfold naturally over time is the best way to put things in perspective and avoid speed bumps in your romantic life. They are itching to move forward with you, and that is great for your confidence.

Couples express energy, which is versatile, determined, and capable. You show others your leadership abilities. You are intelligent, courageous, idealistic, and determined. You obtain a balance between your emotions, and your loyalty to another is steadfast and unquestionable. Finding the correct outlet for your restless spirit improves your emotional well-being. You have an incredible knack for looking to the future and spotting lucky trends to develop. This enables you to accept new potential in your world. You seek more profound challenges and involve yourself more with new activities which inspire your mind. You do best when you are productive and busy. You are advised to beware of drifting and dreaming, set practical goals, and you will achieve them. This is a month which improves stability and obtains proven results.

## ISSUES & HURDLES

You enter a phase of transformation, there are some significant changes indicated which will sweep away negativity, releasing outworn thoughts and modes. You come this time to encourage growth and self-expression. It ultimately sees the ending of one phase, which then makes way for a new cycle to emerge. To benefit fully, you should remain open to new opportunities, as you are being given a chance to achieve significant growth and learning. You may feel under pressure as deadlines are looming, which feel overbearing. The end is coming to a stressful phase, one last push is required to enter a new chapter of potential. You hold the key to a new cycle, life moves towards a new beginning, which contains the promise of a brighter future. Action shapes destiny. You head back to the drawing board to strengthen your closest ties. No cutting corners or skipping steps, as putting in your energy will enable you to build a strong foundation. This helps you shake free of disappointment, it directs you to feel grounded again, owning your true worth draws confidence into your world. Opportunity is coming, open the gateway, and embrace a new chapter of potential. It does suggest that this is a necessary transition to a happier section. Part of this process is letting go, moving away from a situation which causes you great sadness. You can expect developments to arise soon, which give you a clear understanding of the path ahead. The wheels are in motion, and you overcome personal challenges with a sense of flexibility, and fluidity. Being mindful of the complexities of this situation brings balance.

# JULY HOROSCOPE

## ASTROLOGICAL THEME & ZODIAC ENERGY

OBSERVANT ~ HONEST ~ ADVENTUROUS

## WORK & CAREER

You can expect developments in the area of business growth. As you map out new possibilities to explore, you mostly envision a trajectory which is more in alignment with your core goals. This underscores an atmosphere of change, which is cathartic, it removes outworn layers and has a powerful ability to heal old patterns. As you explore a variety of options, it puts you in touch with a sense of freedom, which is exhilarating. You are ready to nurture a new area, a wave of further information arrives to inspire you towards change. As you switch your talents towards an original path, you draw an opportunity to grow and learn in an area which holds promise. This takes your potential to the next level, your gifts are expanding, which is essential for facilitating growth and success. You glide into an opportunity which has your name on it in bold letters. You are ready to lift the lid on a new chapter of potential. Your inspiration is shining brightly, you are being guided to look at long-term goals and determine whether they are still in alignment with your core vision. It is time to broaden your horizons and explore an especially uplifting path. Your fiery optimism searches for the right fit, finding your passion revolutionizes your situation. It takes you forward to a happy chapter. You take advantage of an offer to grow your talents. The universe is gifting you this chance to shine and evolve to a new episode of potential. It heralds a mind-expanding phase, which shines a light on lively discussions and group activities. This draws a sense of abundance into your world, you feel this is the beginning of a constructive rejuvenation of potential. You can look forward to a turbocharged phase which sees you planning to reach your dreams.

## LOVE & ROMANCE

Singles may find that a chance encounter culminates in a time of transformation. It illuminates the potential of a new joint venture. A sense of intimacy pervades your life, it is especially potent because it's the combination of long-held aspirations which have manifested in the most synchronistic manner. Intense emotions could surge as you are especially touched by the affections of another. This is a match which draws abundance into your world. Your life takes a tantalizing turn for the better, you stop living in limbo. A fantastic moment sees you let down your guard with another and become vulnerable. This chance encounter could seal the deal on one of the most important chapters of your life. A vital bond is set to open a flood of abundance into your world. This meeting could be an all or nothing turning point, moving toward happiness and adventure. Exciting times ahead, a chance occurrence opens your eyes to a new situation. Life of blossoms into a truly potent chapter of transformation. What comes together after this meeting is a chapter of discovery. It heralds a new dawn of potential weaving its energy of a manifestation into your world.

Couples reveal their passions are ignited by a new abundance of exciting energy. This is a time of heightened communication and bonding of kindred souls. This foretells of an emerging theme of synchronistic events occurring in your life. Fortuitous opportunities, sharp moves, and the chance to honor your gifts are coming. The universe is asking you to become bolder and move out of your usual routine. What is happening in your world is pure gold and gives you plenty of enthusiasm to embrace. This potential shines a light on your adventurous spirit and captures your heart with its energy.

### IDEAS & CREATIVITY

Soon enough, you find an area to channel your creative energy into. This represents beginning a chapter which resonates strength and power. You are bold, confident, and courageous, able to make things happen. This energy encourages you to capture the essence of willpower and design your life to one of your own makings. You lead with your heart and open yourself up to experiences and people who capture your attention. Opening the book on a new chapter of potential is possible for you soon. This relates to developing a dream of yours, you gather all the information required, and begin to plot a course towards a substantial destination.

Additionally, important news arrives, which gives you valuable information about how to make this vision come together practically. This relates to maintaining stability throughout a phase of growth. There are power and strength in your spirit, this gives you the determination to put your grand ideas out there, this is a lucky time which rockets through your life and helps you create your visionary plans in the physical realm. You capitalize on your talents, this brings you in contact with a support system that encourages your ideas. You crave lively discussions with like-minded folk, this draws inspiring people into your social environment. You can take advantage of your natural talents. You make a bold move when the time is right, and you may also feel inspired to learn more about the new area which captures your attention soon. Expanding your horizons provides an environment which is ripe for artistic potential. You make new friends and invite success into your world with a flourish.

## ISSUES & HURDLES

The past still has a powerful impact on your current situation. You may be feeling pulled in too many directions at this time, your alignment is echoing past vibrations. Taking time to resolve conflicting energy will enable you to address any old emotions which trigger sensitivities. A significant aspect is occurring for you soon, this unfurls a new opportunity in your personal life. It tempts you to take a leap of faith and be bold about future possibilities. This puts you in contact with a variety of people. It allows you to thrive in a new element. Expanding your Horizons sees you seek opportunities which enable you to grow. It plants the seeds for a powerful chapter which unfolds over the coming months. You are being tempted to establish a new area which provides you with a stable platform from which to grow your talents. You have to make some tough decisions which ultimately take you on a path of enlightenment. The trials you have been dealt take you to a phase of growth and rekindle a sense of strength within you. This gives you the extra push to face the future with a brave-heart, you mobilize your talents and can head towards a happier chapter. Life holds a sweet surprise for you soon and helps bring joy into your surroundings. You may have a sense of déjà vu around you, this connects you to a feeling of creativity, which is a reflection of past events, seeking to express themselves currently in your world. Currently. Your cosmic birthright is of an empowering trailblazer. You become open to new opportunities which enable you to grow your talents creatively and spiritually.

# AUGUST HOROSCOPE

## ASTROLOGICAL THEME & ZODIAC ENERGY

COMMITTED ~ IDEALISTIC ~ INSPIRATIONAL

## WORK & CAREER

You enter a new landscape. This Vista lights up incredible potential. It frees your spirit from past limitations, you take a path less traveled and prioritize heading out on new adventures. Moving out of your usual routine prompts you to be at the right time and place for this potential to connect with you. Being conscious of your long-term hopes enables you to make the most of a fresh opportunity. You settle into this new role, finding your groove allows things to come together. It no longer feels like you are swimming upstream. This sees the day-to-day aspects feel more comfortable and adds up to improving your overall quality-of-life. Seeing the positive impact this has on your confidence levels, you begin to feel happy about being able to grow and learn in an area which has taken you out of your comfort zone. Wheels of positivity are turning in your favor.

## LOVE & ROMANCE

It is likely to be a momentous month for your personal life. You go through a cycle which harmonizes your love life, it creates a sense of abundance as you draw a situation into your heart, which offers a great deal of promise. This puts you in touch with an environment of love and expansion. Sweeping changes ahead arrive to revolutionize the potential in your love life. This reshuffles everything, it takes you towards a time where you can feel more secure and begin to plan for future growth. Something which has hindered progress is released to make way for a new flow of abundance. A decisive decision is required to unlock the key to healing a situation with another. This leads to a chapter which emphasizes deepening an emotional bond. You can expect developments in your life in an area which is linked to personal growth. This sets the stage for a more prosperous phase to open in your world soon. It is closely related to emotional well-being. Exploring opportunities which cross your path will heighten the potential in your situation. Don't be shy about seeking support. It does take you towards growth and self-development. It enables you to obtain the right direction for your case. A theme of abundance, security, and happiness arrives to help support you on this journey. Taking a proactive approach is going to pay dividends, reaching out to discuss your concerns will provide you with new tools and abilities you can utilize to improve and ground your energy.

## IDEAS & CREATIVITY

There is a light shining on your energy, which sees things improving for you soon. Something is circulating nicely for you in the background, this brews up new potential in your world. A hidden gem is quickly revealed, this shines a light on an area which has previously been undeveloped. Your budding talents are set to shine in this area soon. Reflecting on the past lets, you fully appreciate how remarkable this journey has been. You have an incredible ability to understand life on a deeper level, your gifts are leading you on a path which does show significant promise. Your spiritual leanings are likely to see you through to a phase which takes you to a valuable breakthrough. The healing that takes place draws new life into your spirit, this is a salve which allows you to transition to a happier phase. You are doing the right thing by reaching for your dreams. Taking proactive steps to obtain a high result is allowing you to listen to your gut instincts, it emphasizes developing an area which can provide you with substantial growth. Improving your surroundings is a strong theme for you, as you shine a light on the potential possible, you move in alignment with your most authentic values. It's an ideal time to structure a course of action, to focus on obtaining a trajectory from where you are now to your future dreams. You can shift out of your comfort zone and embrace a more full world of opportunity. Good news is coming soon to guide your path. You adopt time with your nearest and dearest soon.

## ISSUES & HURDLES

A significant change is indicated, tearing down old layers which no longer serve your purpose, enables you to form a new foundation. Healing energy is arriving, which will transform your outlook. You will become a warrior, not a worrier. As you become open to healing, you find yourself able to let go of damaging memories. Strengthen your core spirit by connecting with your true self. You are headed towards positive change. You have a strong desire to communicate with a sense of purpose in your life, and you are making significant changes which will enable progress to be made.

Additionally, quick and resourceful thinking may be needed to prevail under challenging circumstances. As you summon your courage and faith, you become a creative problem solver. This takes you towards liberation and provides hope in the face of adversity. You are capable of overcoming hurdles and creating a harmonious outcome. Tactical thinking allows you to face problems and succeed in your endeavors. This paves the way for an exciting, positive development to occur.

# SEPTEMBER HOROSCOPE

## ASTROLOGICAL THEME & ZODIAC ENERGY

EXCITING ~ EMOTIONAL ~ ACTIVE

## WORK & CAREER

This is a time which heralds an essential chapter of expanding opportunity in your situation. You can dive into inspiring goals which offer substantial potential for future growth. This relates to developing an area which is a dream of yours, it isn't always an accessible path, but setting intentions does draw the right conditions into your life. A key event stands out is playing an essential role for you soon. You are doing the best you can, under challenging circumstances. While there is a lot of pressure in your life, you mustn't take on the blame. Information is revealed soon, which will provide you with valuable insight. This begins the process of healing old wounds, it takes you towards a happier chapter. There is a necessary change coming, which will be focused in the area of growth and stability. As you think of the possibilities, you are drawn to a path which highlights learning a new area. The seeds you plant this year will ripen and blossom over the coming months. There is still time to harvest your crop sooner rather than later. Becoming involved in events around you will see your opportunities expand. It takes you to a phase which highlights long-term goals, exciting ideas, and testing the waters. A prominent social gathering is ahead, and this could see you at a turning point. A breakthrough brings you towards a fresh chapter of potential. You own your true feelings, integrate your passions into your life, this will be especially important to your success. Taking a long look at your weaknesses will help you overcome these tendencies to hold back when your correct path lays ahead. Nourishing your gifts will help you realize great fulfillment in your world. It's time to set dreams and aspirations for the coming year.

## LOVE & ROMANCE

There is a terrific potential set to be revealed in your circumstances. You are drawing a situation which is firmly connected to faith and luck. It becomes a beautiful phase of self-development and begins a new cycle of potential. It's also a favorable time to communicate with friends, essential conversations turn over a new area to explore. You can embrace the beautiful changes ahead. You resonate an attractive aura which draws people into your world. As you move forward towards a significant chapter, you see how the energy you resonate has a positive effect on others. There is an opportunity ahead, which takes you networking and mingling with your social circle. You find your priorities shift, this leads towards focusing on your nearest and dearest. Embrace the emotional sanctuary which cocoons your energy, it leads to a time of rejuvenation and gives you a buffer zone from outside distractions. You can take advantage of an opportunity which sweeps in to guide you in a new direction soon. It lifts the bar of what is possible in your world and gives you a glimpse of an exciting chapter ahead. You may feel reflective and introspective soon. This is to do with processing the events of the year, it releases outworn energy and does make space for the new potential to arise quickly after. You delight in a time which involves social engagement, and festivities soon. Significant changes are coming, your vision gains forward momentum. You are focused and enterprising, this draws in a significant opportunity, in the first three months you are bold and determined to make your mark on the year. While the past still has a strong influence over you, it becomes part of a more significant phase of growth and opportunity. This sets the stage for some pretty grand plans to emerge mid-year.

## IDEAS & CREATIVITY

This season is a refreshing change for you. You find that drama is left behind, it spotlights a chapter of passion, creativity, and self-expression. Being mindful not to court controversy enables you to deflect any barbs before they impact you negatively. The energy you resonate is returned to you. This brings a sense of healing and abundance into your world. Taking a break leads you to a phase of rejuvenation. You are capable and resilient. You have a strong ability to change and adapt to situations which cross your path. In fact, the landscape of your everyday life is currently shifting, your passion for adventure will welcome the changes ahead. This begins a new phase of potential, which simmers with emotional depth and joint activities. Sharing communications with another is highlighted. You can expect life to change exponentially soon. These changes are positive in nature, it enables the flow of creativity to reach you. Motivation, optimism, and inspiration surge, you are ready to create the life of your dreams. You have untapped talents, the bold, grasp the reins, ride that horse towards your highest destination. You enter an auspicious chapter to support this

29

phase. Expanding your Horizons draws lovely things into your surroundings. You are likely to advance a long-term goal, this shines a light on creativity, and an influx of potential arrives to support your vision. Getting involved in an area which captures your imagination provide you with a powerful outlet for your restless spirit. Everything changes quickly, you find a life picks up the pace, the whirlwind of activity is a positive sign to keep gaining momentum on your dreams.

## ISSUES & HURDLES

The main hurdle for you this month is a fear of failure. This must be overcome for you to progress further. Fear is irrational in nature and does not necessarily reflect the exact situation. It touches on your most instinctive worries, and these deep, unfathomable, and illogical instincts make obstacles out of thin air. You have the courage and stamina to deal with hurdles and overcome obstacles. You are being guided to release the fear and tension this month, and you will be rewarded with a more significant personal platform of stability and equilibrium.

This month will require your skills of problem-solving, as you harness energetic and creative thinking to come up with dynamic solutions. Forge through unknown territory, as you cut away entanglements, use your keen insight to overcome obstacles in your path. You are ethical, perceptive, strategic, and analytics this month. You change direction rapidly, as you develop fresh ideas while rejecting concepts that no longer are valid to your situation. This versatility allows you to see all aspects of the issue at hand, and by using your keen creative mental clarity, you objectively blaze your way through to the heart of the situation. This gives a clear understanding of an issue which makes itself known, which requires you to dispel doubts decisively to find your way back on the level ground once again.

# OCTOBER HOROSCOPE

## ASTROLOGICAL THEME & ZODIAC ENERGY

CAREFUL ~ ~ METHODICAL ~ OBSERVANT

## WORK & CAREER

There are going to be many positive aspects arriving for you soon. It also liberates your spirit, and as you head towards change, you enter a phase of healing, closure, and resolution. This touches many aspects of your life which have clung to your energy, limited your progress, and have not served your higher purpose. As you deal with this time, you create space for a fresh surge of potential to flow into your world. You are likely to unleash your talents in an area which holds promise. This begins a theme of unscripted adventures, you focus on a game-changing area. This combines cosmic energy with your personal intuition. It leads to an expressive chapter which has a heavy focus on self-development. Sudden changes sweep in with the potent and positive force of manifestation. She says the following your urges will take you to the correct path forward. It is a direction which offers you progression, it is likely to see an upgrade occur in your social life. This helps you let down your guard and become open to spending time with someone new. Prepare for some changes around friendships and collaborations, communication arrives to tempt you out in your broader community. This brings a unique perspective into play, shedding outworn values leads to a chapter which illuminates growth. Once you work through the learning curve, you remove draining emotions which have limited your progress. A sense of confidence and capability arrives to hedge you towards favorable outcomes. This helps resolve any doubts you may currently have, avoiding stress is also part of this process. You stoke the fires of inspiration and find the rough edges smooth out over the coming weeks. Stepping up and becoming more involved leads to heightened productivity.

## LOVE & ROMANCE

You are likely to draw several enticing options into your life soon. This heightens the potential in your personal situation, and your intuition will be fundamental in helping guide your path. A particular dynamic with an engaging character becomes intriguing. The chemistry is palpable and sets the stage for some intense moments. You find the dialogue is intelligent and lively. This is someone you can enjoy spending time with. Your dedication and perseverance will see you come out on top. You find your groove and awaken to a bounty of potential which sets your imagination free. This allows you to enter uncharted waters and take in a good dose of happiness. An invitation to develop intimacy with another gives you a tremendous drive to build solid foundations. Creating a solid understanding of this person is an effective way to establish a connection. You are drawing the right situation into your life, the inner or work you do during this process is fundamental in opening your heart fully to the potential which seeks to emerge in your life. Trusting yourself enough to follow your heart is the catalyst which allows you to immerse yourself in an area that creates abundance in your life. Freeing yourself from intellectual constraints which hamper your thinking is beneficial to this process.

## IDEAS & CREATIVITY

Opportunity favors the bold, you shine a light on new potential, you can expect the unexpected as there could be news which arrives swiftly to encourage you out of your comfort zone. This brings manifestations and transitions to the forefront of your awareness. A whole new attitude could emerge as you embrace this potential. Your active and creative mind gets the chance to shine as you express yourself authentically to another. You are ready to follow your dreams. Your priorities may shift away from certain people in your social circle, and as you drift away from these characters, you draw new potential into your life. Forward-thinking people arrive at inspiring you creatively, this encourages you to move forward in a new direction which is more in alignment with your most authentic vision for the future.

## ISSUES & HURDLES

There have been some issues which were not helping your situation. Digging deeper, going within, you find a path which puts you in alignment with a higher trajectory. Impressive results can be obtained, your willingness to open yourself to new environments is instrumental in drawing the right situation into your world. You begin to see signs that have you feeling optimistic, as you nurture this energy, you can focus on achieving a significant personal goal. Flexibility and an open heart let you overcome your own challenges. You have been entering a critical transition, and this does see your situation head toward a beneficial chapter. Fundamental changes are coming, which will reward you with solutions and opportunities for growth. As you navigate your way through the dark territory, you begin to get the sense that you have a handle on this, you can improve your foundations. This week rings in new opportunities for you. It takes you towards expansion, you may even launch a ground-breaking endeavor, which sees you explore a more full world of possibilities. As you illuminate the potential possible, you draw stabilizing energy into your life. You can welcome blessings which tempt you to expand your horizons. A surge of optimism flows into your world soon. News arrives to guide your path. You place a focus on your friendships and collaborations, this is a time where support is essential in your more full circle of friends. Take advantage of opportunities to socialize, this can translate into a phase which draws joy and abundance into your world. Use every available opportunity to create a stable platform from which to grow your new chapter. Putting yourself out in the community, drawing abundance into your world, makes his heart sing.

# NOVEMBER HOROSCOPE

## ASTROLOGICAL THEME & ZODIAC ENERGY

LIVELY ~ INFLUENTIAL ~ IRREPRESSIBLE

## WORK & CAREER

Focus and attention to detail will pay the highest dividends for your working projects. There is a vibe around your energy, which suggests some attractive opportunities are ready to flow into your life. You may be wondering if you are prepared to start a new chapter, but having done the learning necessary, you are now ready to embrace the development of career goals. A new placement is ahead, which gives you a boost. You are right to fiercely protect your bond with another. As you focus on developing long-term goals, you bring all kinds of luck in your world. This charts success and brings you to a time of growth and benefits. You have built rock-solid foundations, and this brings a dazzling sense of brilliance into your world. Taking time to relax and reconnect with the one you love is beneficial for you also. You demonstrate the ability to think on your feet when a new offer reaches you soon. While reaching for this dream takes you out of your comfort zone, it brings with it many blessings for personal growth. Happy news via someone from your past is also likely to cross your path soon. It is a time of renewing bonds and friendships, mingling with people who hold value to you brings great joy into your world. This is going to be an important month for you. Primarily, you will see improvement in an area that has been concerning you recently. It brings powerful creative potential into your world and sets the stage for a fantastic holiday season ahead. You will do exceptionally well through the busy phase. An increase in luck and blessings will also provide you with a chance to grow in a new area.

## LOVE & ROMANCE

You are set to benefit from an enticing new chapter in love and romance. Focusing on developing your goals does see an incredible surge of potential entry into your life. You peel back the layers and get to the heart of the matter with another who captures your attention. Honoring a new chapter with this someone special puts you in touch with your most profound dreams. It does see you opening your heart to a situation which offers many possibilities. There is exciting potential brewing in the background of your personal life. You may have been through an unpredictable time recently, you don't need to worry about that, as improvements are on the way. These beneficial changes will help you glimpse the significant potential which is available in your life. You are being supported by those in spirit to make the best choices possible for your situation. Clearing old emotions paves the way for something special to arrive.

## IDEAS & CREATIVITY

A great deal of stability is available to you. You can appreciate what your efforts this year have achieved. Your dreams are holding steady, new inspiration seeps into your fertile imagination, it's a timely coincidence, as it is a chapter of planning for future growth. This kicks off a cycle of expansion, which begins in the New Year. You are at the height of your creativity, and this holds you in good stead. This is an appropriate time of year to set intentions. An opportunity is ahead, which enables you to study, learn, and launch into a new venture. Don't be hesitant, take a chance, be bold. It is a great time which illuminates essential potential. The crux of this lies in your creativity and willingness to develop your talents. Dusting cobwebs of your inspiration you see motivation is ready to return. You are prepared to contribute essential gifts to a broader audience. The important news is set to arrive, which will illuminate a path forward. This becomes part of a more significant phase, which takes you towards a beneficial chapter. You are ready to make some changes to your situation. Your innovative ideas will provide you with a solution. As you strengthen your confidence, you arrive at a crossroads which compels you to make a final choice. You are currently heading towards a happier chapter, you attend an event where you are surrounded by a crew of positive thinkers. This brings harmony into your world, you are with those who make you feel valued and appreciated. Significant changes are coming for you, you enter a phase where you bright space to bring a resolution to outworn energy and make room for new growth to occur.

## ISSUES & HURDLES

You find yourself having to fight against oppressive and tyrannical energy this month. You stand up to intolerant and narcissistic people by creating a high barrier of defense. Your power is spectacular, fearless, and you express unwavering confidence in your convictions this month. You will not be persuaded by your goals by those who seek to dominate your energy. You fight this intolerant and harsh situation with a sense of daring, and originality. Harness your warrior spirit, and face those who oppose you, along with life's challenges boldly and courageously.

This is not a good month to be inconsistent. A brilliant and concise way forward must be obtained for you to delve into your untapped energies and see progress. Do not be drawn into impractical, inefficient, and whimsical solutions. Apathy will lead to stagnating, so persistent work is needed for your inspirations to manifest. Beware of quick-fix solutions this month, as they are not the solution they first appear to be.

# DECEMBER HOROSCOPE

## ASTROLOGICAL THEME & ZODIAC ENERGY

CURIOUS ~ KNOWLEDGEABLE ~ CHARMING

## WORK & CAREER

New opportunities burn in your life. Soon, this amplifies your ability to achieve a pleasing result. It involves developing your skills and talents and does harness the power of innovation, which brings energy into your world through a surge in your creativity. You initiate new projects and set plans into motion which unfold beautifully for you over the coming months. You make a pilgrimage to a new chapter you flip the switch on an area which begs to be developed. This puts your goal on the front burner and enables you to establish yourself in a position which is perfect for your talents. You enter an inspirational new role which helps cement your foundation in this area. It is the catalyst for incredible growth and does draw ambition into focus. Seeds you plant now come together with a flourish for you to appreciate.

## LOVE & ROMANCE

Someone new and tempting arrives to breathe fresh air into your social life. This is music to your spirit, you find the energy soon intensifies and develops into simmering chemistry. Bracing yourself for a new opportunity sets the stage for the development of emotional bonds. As you unite in companionship with this one, it brings you to a moment which is refreshing and abundant. This takes you to a chapter which is transforming and healing. You are on the right path to achieving your vision. While things may not move as swiftly as you had hoped, you are entering a time which shines a light on the deepening of bonds through a shared group activity. You meet one who inspires you with their generous nature, there are opportunities to spend time with this one, it leads to a joint venture, and this collaboration soon begins to take on a life of its own. Making space for a new chapter enables you to greet the future with an open heart. You no longer are held back by the past and its hold on your spirit. In fact, there is someone special coming into your life, this one puts you in touch with a piece of yourself that you hold sacred. This suggests you are currently transitioning to a far more potent phase of potential. Allow time to catch your breath and appreciate how momentous this journey has been. Any intense feelings you've had in your life recently should begin to lighten up soon. This helps you bright space for a chapter which is joyful and abundant. Regulating the demands on your time will enable you to pace yourself evenly during the hectic phase ahead. There is also an opportunity to begin a new chapter of learning forward.

## IDEAS & CREATIVITY

December is a month which provides you with reflection and insight into the year that been. You begin to see a broader pattern forming about where your life is headed. You have accomplished a great deal this year, curious news is set to arrive which provides you with an enticing path to explore next year. Inspiration flows into your life, which sees you setting grand aspirations for next year. Essential changes are arriving in your world. Watch for a sign which provides you with an important clue. This is going to guide you in the right situation. Being open to new opportunities will let you transition to a happier chapter where you can build an excellent foundation which is grounded and impressive. Stability is the outcome of your patience and flexibility, you are drawing abundance into your surroundings, this sees you benefit from a chapter which is exciting and adventurous. You take matters into your own hands when planning ahead for next year. This provides you with a compelling trajectory which expands the potential available for you. It is a favorable time to upgrade your vision and aim high. You soon become grounded with new responsibilities, this phase of expansion and good fortune is just beginning. As you plan for future growth, it taps into potential, which opens an exciting avenue. Consequently, a more meaningful message is arriving, which allows an understanding that these life changes are guiding you towards the happier chapter. Your gift of empathy and compassion hits the right note with one who makes your heart sing.

## ISSUES & HURDLES

Your tendency to call a spade a spade lands you in hot water this month. You ruffle others feathers easily with your blunt and honest offerings. Sensitive souls easily offended this March, which in turn, causes blocked energy and conflict for you. Trying to develop your skills of diplomacy and tact will help rebalance the voltage and prevent it from becoming a significant hurdle to overcome.

This is a month of expansion and exploration, vision, and creativity. You are being drawn towards new horizons and awakenings, yet these changes can leave you feeling unprepared for the way ahead. It is natural to fear the unknown, and doubt in your ability to develop your life to a whole new level. These concerns can leave you feeling lost and confused, trapped, and confined. But these are merely mental limitations and do not reflect the actual reality of the situation. Allow yourself to surrender to the journey, and accept the flow of your destiny with grace, vision, and trust. Let go of the cliff, and ye shall fly.

The December 22nd Solstice sees a blocked situation in your life is drawing to a close. The removal of old energy will create a position that allows new opportunities to enter into your life.

# ASTROLOGICAL
# DIARY

## 2020

# *Astrological Diary 2020*

## Copyright © 2019 Mystic Cat

Time is set to Coordinated Universal Time Zone (UT±0)

# January

**Mon 30**

**Tues 31**

**Wed 1**
New Year's Day

**Thurs 2**

# January

### Fri 3

First Quarter Moon in Aries. 4.45 UTC
Quadrantids Meteor Shower. Jan 1st-5th. Peaks night of Jan 3rd.

### Sat 4

### Sun 5

### Notes

Lucky Numbers: 11, 62, 12, 61, 32, 5
Astrological Energy: Experiential
Color: White

# January

**Mon 6**

**Tues 7**

**Wed 8**

**Thurs 9**

# January

## Fri 10

Full Moon in Cancer. Wolf Moon. 19:21 UTC
Penumbral Lunar Eclipse.

## Sat 11

## Sun 12

## Notes

Lucky Numbers: 23, 30, 22, 15, 27, 11
Astrological Energy: Directed
Color: Bone

# January

**Mon 13**

**Tues 14**

**Wed 15**

**Thurs 16**

# January

## Fri 17

Last Quarter Moon in Libra. 12.58 UTC

## Sat 18

## Sun 19

## Notes

Lucky Numbers: 32, 88, 26, 40, 92, 85
Astrological Energy: Optimistic
Color: Sky Blue

# January

**Mon 20**

Martin Luther King Day

**Tues 21**

**Wed 22**

**Thurs 23**

# January

## Fri 24
New Moon in Capricorn. 21:42 UTC

## Sat 25
Chinese New Year (Rat)

## Sun 26
Last Quarter Moon in Scorpio.  21.10 UTC

## Notes
Lucky Numbers: 27, 95, 10, 77, 23, 2
Astrological Energy: Visionary
Color: Indigo

# January

**Mon 27**

**Tues 28**

**Weds 29**

**Thurs 30**

# January/February

## Fri 31

## Sat 1

Imbolc

## Sun 2

First Quarter Moon in Taurus. 1.42 UTC.
Groundhog Day

## Notes

Lucky Numbers: 80, 11, 88, 22, 68, 99
Astrological Energy: Influential
Color: Violet

# February

Mon 3

Tues 4

Weds 5

Thurs 6

# February

## Fri 7

## Sat 8

## Sun 9

Full Moon in Leo, Supermoon. Snow Moon. 7:33 UTC

## Notes

Lucky Numbers: 31, 16, 96, 44, 21, 26
Astrological Energy: Commanding
Color: Midnight Blue

# February

## Mon 10
Mercury at largest Eastern Elongation.

## Tues 11

## Weds 12

## Thurs 13

# February

## Fri 14

Valentine's Day

## Sat 15

Last Quarter Moon in Scorpio. 22.17 UTC

## Sun 16

## Notes

Lucky Numbers: 93, 70, 24, 17, 39, 52
Astrological Energy: Imaginative
Color: Royal Blue

# February

## Mon 17

Presidents' Day

## Tues 18

Mercury Retrograde begins

## Weds 19

## Thurs 20

# February

## Fri 21

## Sat 22

## Sun 23
New Moon in Aquarius. 15:32 UTC

## Notes
Lucky Numbers: 49, 52, 8, 43, 85, 76
Astrological Energy: Adventurous
Color: Gold

# February

**Mon 24**

**Tues 25**
Shrove Tuesday (Mardi Gras)

**Weds 26**
Ash Wednesday

**Thurs 27**

# February/March

## Fri 28

## Sat 29

## Sun 1

## Notes

Lucky Numbers: 24, 67, 64, 94, 96, 55
Astrological Energy: Vivacious
Color: Yellow

# March

## Mon 2

First Quarter Moon in Gemini. 19.57 UTC

## Tues 3

## Weds 4

## Thurs 5

# March

**Fri 6**

**Sat 7**

**Sun 8**

## Notes

Lucky Numbers: 84, 50, 93, 9, 48, 8
Astrological Energy: Productive
Color: Hot Pink

# March

## Mon 9

Full Moon in Virgo, Supermoon. Worm Moon. 17:48 UTC
Mercury Retrograde ends.
Purim (begins at sundown)

## Tues 10

Purim (ends at sundown)

## Weds 11

## Thurs 12

# March

## Fri 13

## Sat 14

## Sun 15

## Notes

Lucky Numbers: 27, 62, 37, 49, 90, 69
Astrological Energy: Passionate
Color: Cyan

# March

## Mon 16
Last Quarter Moon in Sagittarius. 9.34 UTC

## Tues 17
St Patrick's Day

## Wed 18

## Thurs 19

# March

## Fri 20

Ostara/Spring Equinox. 3:50 UTC

## Sat 21

## Sun 22

## Notes

Lucky Numbers: 74, 38, 95, 88, 2, 72
Astrological Energy: Constructive
Color: Spring Green

# March

## Mon 23

## Tues 24

Mercury at most substantial Western Elongation.
Venus at most substantial Eastern Elongation.
New Moon in Aries. 9:28 UTC

## Weds 25

## Thurs 26

# March

**Fri 27**

**Sat 28**

**Sun 29**

**Notes**

Lucky Numbers: 3, 93, 58, 91, 27, 81
Astrological Energy: Trusting
Color: Rose

# March/April

**Mon 30**

**Tues 31**

**Weds 1**

First Quarter Moon in Cancer. 10.21 UTC
All Fools/April Fools Day

**Thurs 2**

# April

## Fri 3

## Sat 4

## Sun 5
Palm Sunday

## Notes
Lucky Numbers: 3, 66, 5, 74, 53, 82
Astrological Energy: Celebratory
Color: Lemon

# April

## Mon 6

## Tues 7

## Weds 8

Full Moon in Libra, Supermoon. Pink Moon. 2:35 UTC
Passover (begins at sunset)

## Thurs 9

# April

## Fri 10
Good Friday

## Sat 11

## Sun 12
Easter Sunday

## Notes
Lucky Numbers: 86, 33, 34, 35, 75, 61
Astrological Energy: Harmonious
Color: Amber

# April

## Mon 13

## Tues 14

Last Quarter Moon in Capricorn. 22.56 UTC

## Weds 15

## Thurs 16

Passover ends

# April

## Fri 17
Orthodox Good Friday

## Sat 18

## Sun 19
Orthodox Easter

## Notes
Lucky Numbers: 37, 65, 90, 62, 99, 5
Astrological Energy: Inspiring
Color: Baby Blue

# April

## Mon 20

## Tues 21

## Weds 22

Lyrids Meteor Shower. April 16th-25th. Peaks night of April 22nd.
Earth Day

## Thurs 23

New Moon in Taurus. 2:26 UTC
Ramadan Begins

# April

## Fri 24

## Sat 25

## Sun 26

## Notes

Lucky Numbers: 88, 39, 83, 85, 26, 28
Astrological Energy: Committed
Color: Honeydew

# April

## Mon 27

## Tues 28

## Weds 29

## Thurs 30
First Quarter Moon in Leo. 20.38 UTC

# May

## Fri 1

Beltane/May Day

## Sat 2

## Sun 3

## Notes

Lucky Numbers: 18, 15, 51, 13, 41, 1
Astrological Energy: Complex
Color: Deep Pink

# May

## Mon 4

## Tues 5

## Weds 6

Eta Aquarids Meteor Shower. April 19th - May 28th. Peaks night of May 6th.

## Thurs 7

Full Moon in Scorpio, Supermoon. Flower Moon. 10:45 UTC

# May

## Fri 8

## Sat 9

## Sun 10
Mother's Day

## Notes
Lucky Numbers: 43, 65, 59, 5, 54, 34
Astrological Energy: Productive
Color: Forest Green

# May

## Mon 11

## Tues 12

## Weds 13

## Thurs 14

Last Quarter Moon in Aquarius. 14.03 UTC

# May

## Fri 15

## Sat 16

## Sun 17

## Notes

Lucky Numbers: 11, 68, 9, 39, 20, 88
Astrological Energy: Vibrant
Color: Aqua

# May

**Mon 18**

Victoria Day (Canada)

**Tues 19**

**Weds 20**

**Thurs 21**

# May

## Fri 22

New Moon in Taurus. 17:39 UTC

## Sat 23

Ramadan Ends

## Sun 24

## Notes

Lucky Numbers: 81, 34, 21, 97, 66, 43
Astrological Energy: Courageous
Color: Dark Violet

# May

**Mon 25**

Memorial Day

**Tues 26**

**Weds 27**

**Thurs 28**

Shavuot (begins at sunset)

# May

## Fri 29

## Sat 30

First Quarter Moon in Virgo. 3.30 UTC
Shavuot (ends at sunset)

## Sun 31

## Notes

Lucky Numbers: 29, 85, 92, 91, 60, 30
Astrological Energy: Complex
Color: Slate Blue

# June

## Mon 1

## Tues 2

## Weds 3

## Thurs 4

Mercury at Greatest Eastern Elongation.

# June

### Fri 5

Full Moon in Sagittarius. Strawberry Moon. 19:12 UTC
Penumbral Lunar Eclipse.

### Sat 6

### Sun 7

### Notes

Lucky Numbers: 74, 57, 56, 75, 67, 33
Astrological Energy: Daring
Color: Straw

# June

## Mon 8

## Tues 9

## Weds 10
Jupiter at Opposition.

## Thurs 11

# June

## Fri 12

## Sat 13

Last Quarter Moon in Pisces. 6.24 UTC

## Sun 14

Flag Day

## Notes

Lucky Numbers: 24, 61, 96, 42, 88, 47
Astrological Energy: Active
Color: Fire Brick

# June

## Mon 15

## Tues 16

## Weds 17
Mercury Retrograde begins.

## Thurs 18

# June

## Fri 19

## Sat 20

## Sun 21

New Moon in Cancer. 6:41 UTC
Midsummer/Litha Solstice. 21:44 UTC
Annual Solar Eclipse.
Father's Day

## Notes

Lucky Numbers: 21, 96, 92, 61, 36, 70
Astrological Energy: Exciting
Color: Cornflower Blue

# June

Mon 22

Tues 23

Weds 24

Thurs 25

# June

**Fri 26**

**Sat 27**

**Sun 28**
First Quarter Moon in Libra. 8.16 UTC

**Notes**
Lucky Numbers: 5, 91, 69, 39, 64, 6
Astrological Energy: Creative
Color: Red

# June/July

**Mon 29**

**Tues 30**

**Weds 1**
Canada Day

**Thurs 2**

# July

## Fri 3
Independence Day (observed)

## Sat 4
Independence Day

## Sun 5
Full Moon in Capricorn. Buck Moon 4:44 UTC
Penumbral Lunar Eclipse.

## Notes
Lucky Numbers: 58, 40, 99, 95, 18, 92
Astrological Energy: Curious
Color: Orange

# July

**Mon 6**

**Tues 7**

**Weds 8**

**Thurs 9**

# July

## Fri 10

## Sat 11

## Sun 12

Last Quarter Moon in Aries. 23.29 UTC
Mercury Retrograde ends.

## Notes

Lucky Numbers: 7, 36, 2, 20, 98 77
Astrological Energy: Stimulating
Color: Crimson

# July

## Mon 13

## Tues 14
Jupiter at Opposition.

## Weds 15

## Thurs 16

# July

## Fri 17

## Sat 18

## Sun 19

## Notes

Lucky Numbers: 82, 42, 66, 87, 42, 58
Astrological Energy: Inventive
Color: Ruby

# July

## Mon 20
New Moon in Cancer. 17:33 UTC
Saturn at Opposition.

## Tues 21

## Weds 22
Mercury at Greatest Western Elongation.

## Thurs 23

# July

## Fri 24

## Sat 25

## Sun 26

## Notes

Lucky Numbers: 31, 46, 25, 23, 43, 37
Astrological Energy: Methodical
Color: Peach

# July/August

**Mon 27**

First Quarter Moon in Scorpio. 12.32 UTC

**Tues 28**

Delta Aquarids Meteor Shower. July 12th – Aug 23rd. Peaks night of July 28th.

**Weds 29**

**Thurs 30**

# July/August

## Fri 31

## Sat 1
Lammas/Lughnasadh

## Sun 2

## Notes
Lucky Numbers: 35, 1, 7, 53, 26, 51
Astrological Energy: Constructive
Color: Lavender

# August

## Mon 3
Full Moon in Aquarius. Sturgeon Moon. 15:59 UTC

## Tue 4

## Wed 5

## Thurs 6

# August

**Sat 8**

**Sun 9**

## Notes

Lucky Numbers: 30, 76, 90, 8, 41, 21
Astrological Energy: Independent
Color: Scarlet

# August

## Mon 10

## Tues 11

Last Quarter Moon in Taurus. 16.45 UTC.

## Weds 12

Perseids Meteor Shower. July 17th to August 24th. Peaks night of Aug 12th.

## Thurs 13

Venus at Greatest Western Elongation.

# August

## Fri 14

## Sat 15

## Sun 16

## Notes

Lucky Numbers: 65, 36, 98, 86, 47, 9
Astrological Energy: Aware
Color: Bronze

# August

## Mon 17

## Tues 18

## Weds 19
New Moon in Leo. 2:41 UTC

## Thurs 20
Islamic New Year

# August

**Fri 21**

**Sat 22**

**Sun 23**

## Notes

Lucky Numbers: 40, 33, 63, 37, 45, 56
Astrological Energy: Spirited
Color: Mint

# August

**Mon 24**

**Tues 25**

First Quarter Moon in Scorpio. 17.58 UTC

**Weds 26**

**Thurs 27**

# August

## Fri 28

## Sat 29

## Sun 30

## Notes

Lucky Numbers: 22, 1, 30, 25, 2, 6
Astrological Energy: Enchanting
Color: Turquoise

# August/September

## Mon 31

## Tues 1

## Weds 2
Full Moon in Pisces. Full Corn Moon. 5:22 UTC

## Thurs 3

# September

## Fri 4

## Sat 5

## Sun 6

## Notes

Lucky Numbers: 86, 69, 78, 50, 71, 80
Astrological Energy: Unique
Color: Topaz

# September

## Mon 7

Labor Day

## Tues 8

## Weds 9

## Thurs 10

Last Quarter Moon in Gemini. 9.26 UTC

# September

**Fri 11**

Neptune at Opposition.

**Sat 12**

**Sun 13**

**Notes**

Lucky Numbers: 10, 12, 38, 62, 13, 91
Astrological Energy: Magnetic
Color: Coral

# September

**Mon 14**

**Tues 15**

**Weds 16**

**Thurs 17**
New Moon in Virgo. 11:00 UTC

# September

## Fri 18

Rosh Hashanah (begins at sunset)

## Sat 19

## Sun 20

Rosh Hashanah (ends at sunset)

## Notes

Lucky Numbers: 1, 54, 36, 80, 79, 57
Astrological Energy: Open
Color: White

# September

## Mon 21
International Day of Peace

## Tues 22
Mabon/Fall Equinox. 13:31 UTC

## Weds 23

## Thurs 24
First Quarter Moon in Capricorn. 1.55 UTC

# September

**Fri 25**

**Sat 26**

**Sun 27**

Yom Kippur (begins at sunset)

**Notes**

Lucky Numbers: 53, 89, 92, 97, 79, 71
Astrological Energy: Magical
Color: Maroon

# September/October

## Mon 28
Yom Kippur (ends at sunset)

## Tues 29

## Weds 30

## Thurs 1
Full Moon in Aries. Harvest Moon. 21:05 UTC
Mercury at Greatest Eastern Elongation.

# October

## Fri 2
Sukkot (begins at sunset)

## Sat 3

## Sun 4

## Notes
Lucky Numbers: 42, 11, 26, 5, 82, 14
Astrological Energy: Empathic
Color: Dark Orange

# October

## Mon 5

## Tues 6

## Weds 7

Draconids Meteor Shower. Oct 6th-10th. Peak night of Oct 7th.

## Thurs 8

# October

## Fri 9

Sukkot (ends at sunset)

## Sat 10

Last Quarter Moon in Cancer. 0.39 UTC

## Sun 11

## Notes

Lucky Numbers: 64, 1, 59, 48, 36, 61
Astrological Energy: Organized
Color: Chocolate

# October

## Mon 12

Columbus Day
Thanksgiving Day (Canada)
Indigenous People's Day

## Tues 13

Mercury Retrograde begins.

## Weds 14

## Thurs 15

**Fri 16**

New Moon in Libra. 19:31 UTC

**Sat 17**

**Sun 18**

**Notes**

Lucky Numbers: 49, 37, 22, 78, 8, 4
Astrological Energy: Perceptive
Color: Salmon

# October

**Mon 19**

**Tues 20**

**Weds 21**

Orionids Meteor Shower. Oct 2nd - Nov 7th. Peaks night of Nov 21st.

**Thurs 22**

# October

## Fri 23
First Quarter Moon in Capricorn. 13.23 UTC

## Sat 24

## Sun 25

## Notes
Lucky Numbers: 96, 91, 20, 27, 33, 76
Astrological Energy: Mysterious
Color: Black

# October

**Mon 26**

**Tues 27**

**Weds 28**

**Thurs 29**

## Fri 30

## Sat 31

Full Moon, Blue Moon in Taurus. Hunters Moon. 14:49 UTC
Uranus at Opposition.
Samhain/Halloween.

## Sun 1

All Saints' Day

## Notes

Lucky Numbers: 50, 44, 49, 97, 25, 1
Astrological Energy: Psychic
Color: Midnight

# November

## Mon 2

## Tues 3

Mercury Retrograde ends.

## Weds 4

Taurids Meteor Shower. Sept 7th - Dec 10th. Peaks on Nov 4th.

## Thurs 5

# November

**Fri 6**

**Sat 7**

**Sun 8**

Last Quarter Moon in Leo. 13.46 UTC

**Notes**

Lucky Numbers: 43, 18, 73, 51, 54, 92
Astrological Energy: Profound
Color: Royal Blue

# November

## Mon 9

## Tues 10

## Weds 11

Remembrance Day (Canada)
Veterans Day

## Thurs 12

# November

## Fri 13

## Sat 14

## Sun 15
New Moon in Scorpio. 5:07 UTC

## Notes
Lucky Numbers: 10, 7, 54, 57, 91, 21
Astrological Energy: Hectic
Color: Teal

# November

**Mon 16**

**Tues 17**

Leonids Meteor Shower. Nov 6th-30th. Peaks night of Nov 17th.

**Weds 18**

**Thurs 19**

# November

**Fri 20**

**Sat 21**

**Sun 22**

First Quarter Moon in Pisces. 4.45 UTC

**Notes**

Lucky Numbers: 75, 92, 5, 47, 99, 93
Astrological Energy: Structured
Color: Sky Blue

# November

**Mon 23**

**Tues 24**

**Weds 25**

**Thurs 26**
Thanksgiving Day (US)

# November

## Fri 27

## Sat 28

## Sun 29

## Notes

Lucky Numbers: 7, 25, 52, 75, 67, 55
Astrological Energy: Social
Color: Magenta

# November/December

## Mon 30

Full Moon in Gemini. Beaver Moon. 9:30 UTC
Penumbral Lunar Eclipse.

## Tues 1

## Weds 2

## Thurs 3

# December

Fri 4

Sat 5

Sun 6

## Notes

Lucky Numbers: 87, 3, 92, 14, 83, 13
Astrological Energy: Impulsive
Color: Midnight Blue

# December

## Mon 7

## Tues 8

Last Quarter Moon in Virgo. 0.37 UTC

## Weds 9

## Thurs 10

Hanukkah (begins at sunset)

# December

## Fri 11

## Sat 12

## Sun 13

Geminids Meteor Shower. Dec 7$^{th}$-17$^{th}$. Peaks nights of Dec 13$^{th}$-15$^{th}$.

## Notes

Lucky Numbers: 67, 10, 7, 43, 76, 99
Astrological Energy: Vibrant
Color: Snow

# December

## Mon 14
New Moon in Sagittarius. 16:17 UTC

## Tues 15

## Weds 16

## Thurs 17

# December

## Fri 18
Hanukkah (ends at sunset)

## Sat 19

## Sun 20

## Notes
Lucky Numbers: 16, 85, 10, 96, 67, 1
Astrological Energy: Festive
Color: Powder Blue

# December

## Mon 21

Ursids Meteor Shower. Dec 17th – 25th. Peaks night of Dec 21st.
Great Conjunction of Jupiter and Saturn.
Yule/ Winter Solstice. 10:02 UTC
First Quarter Moon in Pisces. 23.41 UTC

## Tues 22

## Weds 23

## Thurs 24

# December

## Fri 25

Christmas Day

## Sat 26

Boxing Day (Canada & Uk)
Kwanzaa begins

## Sun 27

## Notes

Lucky Numbers: 33, 6, 30, 17, 80, 76
Astrological Energy: Graceful
Color: White

# December

## Mon 28

## Tues 29

## Weds 30
Full Moon in Cancer. Cold Moon. 3:28 UTC

## Thurs 31
New Year's Eve

# January

## Fri 1

New Year's Day
Kwanzaa ends

## Sat 2

## Sun 3

## Notes

Lucky Numbers: 23, 15, 12, 29, 71, 86
Astrological Energy: Aware
Color: Green Yellow

*May the stars shine brightly in your world in 2020, and beyond.*

# About Crystal Sky

Crystal is passionate about the universe, helping others, and personal development. She produces a range of astrologically minded diaries to celebrate the universal forces which affect us all. All reviews are read and appreciated.

Other Titles in the 2020 range:

Fairy Moon Diary 2020: Fairy Messages & Astrological Datebook
Shaman Moon Diary 2020: Shamanic Messages & Astrological Datebook

When not writing about the stars, you can find Crystal under them, gazing up at the abundance that surrounds us all, with her dogs by her side.

11083392R00092

Made in the USA
Monee, IL
05 September 2019